unsent feelings

Gema Garcia

Para Mi Familia:

Words in any language fall short of capturing the depth of my love for you but let this be a start. Thank you for being the gold that kept me together and reminded me of my value. I love you beyond the worn-out phrases, beyond "life itself" and every tired metaphor.

CONTENTS

You've mistaken the heartache for
weakness,
but that thudding in your chest?
That's the sound of rebuilding.

Every break
becomes a blueprint.
Every scar,
a trail to somewhere new.

You think you're crumbling,
but darling,
you're being carved.

Soft things become strong.
Shaken ground settles.

Your heart is not fragile,
Your heart — like you —
is more resilient than you think.

Gema Garcia

Dear Reader,

These poems are a reflection of the growing pains my heart endured this past year. As a result, I've made room for more love and experience.

Each stage of growth is captured in three distinct parts.

The first part is about **breaking and tearing** — the moments of loss, pain, and unlearning.

The second part focuses on **healing and growth** — the slow, steady process of becoming whole again.

The third part is dedicated to **love** — the **gratitude**, warmth, and joy that follow.

Each poem is a step along this journey, weaving together the story of a heart learning to grow bigger, braver, and more open. Sharing these words feels vulnerable, even exposing. Yet, if just one person finds solace in a single line, feels understood, or a little less alone, then it will all have been worth it.

As you read through the process of my healing, I hope it will help your heart heal a little, too.

unsent feelings

the breaking

I was ready this time —
ready to tell you how I felt.

I climbed into your truck
electric with nerves,
but before I could speak,
you told me you'd met someone.

I swallowed the words -
Sharp and jagged
and folded my feelings
back into the box
where they had been waiting for
months.

I tossed it into the backseat
next to patience, self-control,
and every other part of me
you never asked for.

I then reached for my "calm
friend" mask.
It fit so well
you'd think it was made for me.
For 3 hours, I wore it —
I wore it like armor
that didn't protect me.

When you left me
in the parking lot at 1 a.m.,
I took it off,
tearing it from my skin.

I reached back for the box.
The crack of it opening
sounded like my own heart
breaking.

unsent feelings

My friends came to save me
from the weight of my silent
thoughts,
their presence a quiet anchor

the night couldn't tell my tears
from its rain.
We drove, hours slipping by,
words unspoken,
The warmth of a hand on my
shoulder spoke volumes without a
sound.

Each tear sealed together the
broken pieces of nostalgia, joy,
and the bitter crash of reality.

The truck hummed like a lullaby
as dawn's first light brushed the
horizon, and with it,
my view shifted—

the brokenness softened,
and hope unfurled like the new
day.

With the rise of the sun, my heart
rose too,
Reality became a warm embrace,
the weight of the past lifting
as we watched the world wake up.

You were driving my car.
When I glanced at you,
my stomach dropped—
I swore I wouldn't want this.

But I wondered anyway—
what it would be like
to feel something warmer
than the cold kiss of the air.

You met my eyes,
pulled me back—
or was I already gone?

You did nothing wrong —
showed up with fresh daisies,
charmed my family with ease.

I wanted to kiss you,
so I did.
Maybe that was all I wanted.

But now I feel it—
the weight of your quiet;
still waiting.

I wonder
if I'm the one to blame,
using you like that
without knowing—

until I knew.

Time passed, but the moment you
left,
I knew —
It wasn't the kiss that said
goodbye —
it was me.

I tried to convince my mind
that you were right for us,
and for a while,
I almost believed it.

But I forgot
I had a heart and body,
that knew better

For three days, I wandered in a
haze,
wanting to shield you from the
fall, knowing that in the end,

I'd be the one to push us both.

So I did what stung now —

saved us

from a lifetime

of pain.

unsent feelings

I hated

that I made you cry —

but the relief,

sharp and certain,

of listening to my body and spirit

was like a cool breeze

on a humid day,

like the first exhale

after surfacing from deep water —

lungs burning,

but breathing again.

Thank you for loving me
not for who I could be,
but for who I was —
Confused, overwhelmed and trying.

I presented to you a beautiful
glass vase,

a whole family's love in one
place.

You used it with ease until one
day,

while handing it back to me
you dropped it and it shattered
into a million pieces.

Nonchalantly you handed me a
dollar to replace it.

I've seen you since that day

but I've learned not to hand you
anything of value again.

I lost four of you in one week
and no one told me why.

I felt emptied —
as if everything inside me
was quietly stolen.

Tears didn't rebuild me this time.
They wore me down,
like water smoothing stone
to sand.

For seven days,
I wore "fine" on my face at work.
But every evening,
I crumbled in the driver's seat —
headlights catching the wreck of
me,

My head would hit the pillow,
damp from every hour
I had failed to be "fine".

I don't know
what makes it so easy
for those I love
to walk away.

Am I that replaceable?
Like batteries drained —
useful, then useless,
tossed aside without a second
glance.

Was I ever more than convenience?
Or did they only see me
as something that powers them,
until I couldn't anymore?

Just because I forgive you
doesn't mean we return
to your version of "right."

I've always known my worth —
But now,

I know how little
you ever did.

Gema Garcia

You've taken steps back
so gradually,
I'm not sure you've noticed.

We went from daily calls
and seeing each other twice a
week,
to now —
just a passenger on your commute,

You only call from your car,
My name flickers in your mind
only when there's no one else to
fill the silence.

Weeks stretch between us.
I wonder if I'm just
a background station
you don't bother to change.

We weren't torn apart.
You weren't pulled away —
you just stopped holding on.

I watched us become strangers —
not with a bang,
but with a thousand quiet sighs.

I spent months
thinking it through,
crafting a birthday gift
that brought you to tears.

You sent "happy birthday"
at 11:59 —

like I was something

you almost forgot.

That's how I learned
I was an afterthought.

unsent feelings

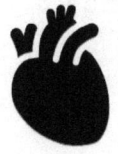

Did you know
I was in love with you?
Or did you think
I just woke up at 3 a.m.
for anyone?

Did you think
I never let my phone
go to voicemail?

That I give gifts
this thoughtful
to everyone?

That I am always this available —

Did you think
my day was so easily made
by anyone
sending me a song?

I gave you
girlfriend treatment.

You gave me
acquaintance treatment.

You never told me
you wanted more than friendship.
You never had to.

But when people asked us,
"Are you two together?"
you stayed quiet.

Not a yes.
Not a no.

Just a silence
that left me to do the talking.
So, I did.

I said,
"No, we're just friends."

I said it like it didn't hurt,
like I didn't want more than that.

But now,
I hear the quiet differently.
It wasn't indecision.

It was permission
to lie to myself.

I wanted to make you feel
comfortable.
I wanted to make you feel
confident.
I wanted to make you feel
chosen.

But somewhere in all that wanting,

I felt uncomfortable.
I felt unworthy.
I felt unseen.

And you
never chose me.

It was a different kind of
intimacy.

You told me
you kissed a girl
before our date.

Then you ran
to my apartment
to tell me
you loved her.

I didn't necessarily
want to be the one
you loved anymore,

but my heart
remembered
when I did.

I'm losing you again,

but this time,

I've stopped calling it a loss.

I'm not losing myself too.

I set you down gently,
and lifted myself up.

I unthreaded you from my heart,
stitching myself in your place.

I walked away from you
and toward me.

I stopped writing love letters to
you
and began putting pen to paper for
myself instead.

the healing

One morning I woke up and the air
felt different.

The weight on my chest had eased,
Breath moved through me without
resistance—

your name wasn't the first thing
to come into my mind

I noticed it slowly,
like light shifting across a room.
No shadow of you lingered in my
thoughts.

Maybe this is what healing feels
like—

a gradual untangling,
a letting go of things
once held too tightly.

There was no thunder, no blaze,
no grand moment of knowing.
It happens in stillness,
in the space between breaths—
a peace that asks for nothing,
but offers everything.

I may not be in your life
anymore,
but I still thank God
that, for a season,
you grew in mine.

I may not sparkle
for you anymore,
but each flicker of light
reminds me —
I was always the flame.

Cry —
not because you allowed it,
but because it arrived,
uninvited,
like rain on a cloudless day.

Let it fall.
It's not weakness,
it's water carving its way out.

Healing isn't polite.
It doesn't knock or wait.
It breaks in,
Like a flood
without permission.

So you cried
when that guy rejected you —
Brave.
That means you let yourself feel
it.

So you loved fully
and it wasn't returned —
beautiful.
because you loved at all.

So you broke down
at the wrong time,
felt too much,
wanted too deeply —
who told you that was wrong?

Own your heart
as it is.
Life's too short
to be embarrassed
by the proof that you cared.

Being true to myself,

I'll bend

like rivers around stone,

carve paths

through resistance —

just to make life softer

for you.

Just keep living
until you're alive again.

Breathe,
even when the air feels heavy.

Walk,
even if every step feels hollow.

The sun will rise
without your permission —
let it.

Seasons will shift
while you sit in the same spot —
notice it.

Healing doesn't ask for witnesses,
it moves quietly,

One day,
without warning,
you'll wake up
and feel it —

a pulse of warmth,
a softness in the once sharp
places.

Keep living
until you're alive again.

Not all beginnings
arrive with fanfare —
some just
begin.

What I felt in the moment

molded me -

but it never claimed me.

I am shaped by the moments I
lived,

not defined by them.

Not all loss is ruin.
What fades is not forgotten —
it is transformed.

Edges soften.
Surfaces smooth.
What was jagged becomes gentle.

Erosion isn't the end.
It's the beginning of something
new.

The land doesn't mourn the
shoreline,
it embraces the sea.

So, let time shape you.
Let it strip away what no longer
fits.
What remains will be raw,
yes —
but it will be beautiful.

When we first met,
you told me
you were a naturally rude person.

I've known you almost a year now,
and I can tell you with certainty
—
you aren't rude.

You are strong
where it matters.

Kind
where it hurts.

Gentle
in ways you don't even see.

The man you let stay
is the reason you think you're
rude.

He fights you,
antagonizes you,
until you fight back —
then, in the same breath,
he reminds you
you're lucky to have him
because you're "rude."

But I have seen you without him.
I pray, one day,
you meet yourself
the way I have.

Not everyone deserves every shade
of me.
Some will only know the dawn,
soft light and quiet warmth.

Others will meet the storm —
all thunder, flash, and downpour.

I am not the same sky for
everyone,
and that's okay.

I'm learning to keep the whole
horizon
for those who see beauty
in every weather.

Kindness is a choice,
not my only setting.

Don't mistake my softness
for surrender.

I have fought to stay this gentle.

If you feel my edge one day,
know this —

even gardens have thorns,
even the ocean has a tide
that pulls back.

My patience, my love, my light
—they have limits
I will not break myself
just to keep you comfortable.

Sometimes I come home,
weary from the day.

look around,
and see my silly little plants
and my silly little books.

I close my eyes,
softened by it all.

I smile,
realizing I'm falling in love
with this quiet little world
I'm building for myself.

Growth is uncomfortable,
embrace it
You are not breaking —
you're blooming.
So, lean into it.
Pain is just the sound
of becoming.

Midway through the flood of
healing,
you resurfaced.

I swore it was over.

But it returned —
not as a river's rush,
but as a steady stream —
soft, unyielding,
like fingers tracing familiar
paths
around my ankles.

I let it swirl
until I remembered —
I know how to stand.

And I did.
Steady again.

unsent feelings

I took a leap beyond my comfort.
It was terrifying.
But here,
I am finally breathing.

Not the shallow gasp of survival
but something deeper,
like my lungs
had been waiting for this air
all along.

This is where my life began —
not in the quiet, padded world of
"safe,"

nor the steady pull of
"predictable,"

but in the beautiful,
unsteady place
just beyond it.

Surround yourself with love —

even if, at first,

it's only your own arms holding
you steady.

Gema Garcia

Take a moment —
not to chase what's next,
but to turn around.

See the path behind you:

The words you tripped over,
but still spoke aloud.
The race you swore you'd never
run,
legs heavy with doubt, breath thin
with fear.
The storms you thought would
swallow you whole.

But here you are.

Not unscathed,
but standing.
Not untouched,
but wiser.

Don't rush this moment.
Breathe it in.

This is growth —
quiet, steady, undeniable.

Do you know the weight of your
luck —

to have me in your life?
I love to love —
freely, wildly,
with no conditions,
no strings to pull me back.

But don't mistake that freedom
for endless supply.

My love is abundant,
but finite

It will be your actions
that determine how much of it
you will continue to hold.

I shouldn't have to brace myself
just to see you —
but I do now.

You call me rude
because I don't respond
with the softness you once knew.

But here's the thing —
I'm at peace with that.
And peace doesn't always sound
polite.

I'm healed enough
to run my fingers
along the gold
that fills my cracks —

not with shame,
but with reverence.

Every fracture,
every break,
every moment I swore
I'd never feel whole again —
they shine now.

I'm grateful to live so fully,
because even the broken parts
still belong to me.

unsent feelings

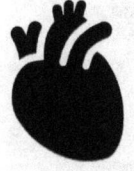

the loving

I choose to dream —
not the quiet, fleeting kind
that drifts away with the dawn,
but the wild, stubborn kind
that grips me until I move.

I choose to turn that dream
into something real —

brick by brick,
breath by breath.
No blueprint,
just belief.

I choose the me
I haven't met yet.

The one waiting on the other side
of fear,
patience in her eyes,
power in her stance

She calls to me,
not with words,
but with the steady rhythm
of becoming.

And step by step,
I am answering her call.

unsent feelings

They say
hurt people hurt people —
wounds passed down
like a chain with no ending.

But you showed me
the other side of that coin.
You taught me that love, too,
can be contagious.

I see it clearly now —
loved people love people.

Thank you
for being the proof.

Acting small serves no one —

not you, not them,

and certainly not the world

that's been waiting for you all
this time.

You were meant to be seen,

And not just by him,

but by every moment that calls
your name.

You were born to take up space —

Fully,

Unapologetically

For so long, I played the
supporting role —
The best friend, the bystander,
the voice with no goal.

I watched from the wings as the
stars stole the show,
Waiting for someone to tell me:
"Go!"

But the camera turned, and I saw —
I'm the one with the pen, the
plot, and the blame,
The credits roll under my name.

No director's commands, no waiting
for cues —
This story is mine, and I get to
choose.
No damsel, no extra, no girl
chasing fame —
I'm rewriting the script, no time
to be tame.

I'll craft every scene with wild,
bold delight,
My triumphs, my heartaches, the
stars of the night.

I'll fall, and I'll rise, I'll
laugh 'til I cry,
I'll dance in the rain, let the
music reply.

Because guess what? It's mine.
Every plot twist, each frame,
every line.

No need for permission, no asking
"Who, me?" —
I'm the leading lady. Just watch.
You'll see.

"A Meet-Cute with My Life"

I wandered through doorways, eyes
chasing a spark,
Hunting for love where the world
felt most dark.

But life stepped in, unannounced
and unplanned —
No plot twist, no pretense, no
script in my hand.

Joy linked its arm with mine like
an old friend returned,
No prince in the story, no cue for
the start —
Just me, and my life, meeting
here, heart-to-heart.

So I stop scanning the crowd for
love at first sight —
Turns out it's me, and it just
feels so right.

Fall in love
with the you that is still
becoming,
the one who changes her mind,
who breaks her own heart
just to see what's inside.

Every version of you
is a home worth returning to.

No need to knock.
No need to wait for permission.

Just step inside.

You're building this house

brick by beautiful brick.

Gema Garcia

What I fear

more than the world's opinion of
me

is the judgment I carry,

the one I can't escape.

Their voices may fade,

but mine echoes loud.

I care more

about the way I see myself

than how the world

chooses to see me.

unsent feelings

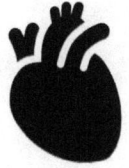

"Dear You"

Thank you for being the first
person I thought to call
while the salt of fresh tears
still clung to my face.

Thank you for bringing more tears
—
not from pain this time,
but from the kind of laughter that
makes your side ache
in the sweetest way.

We don't share blood or lineage,
but what is blood and hair
compared to love?

You have been a mother when I
needed guidance,
a sister when I needed solidarity,
and a best friend, always.

You have been every kind of love I
didn't know I needed.
Thank you for loving me in all my
shapes,
all my moods,
and all my unspoken thoughts.
Know that I love you just as
endlessly.

What if I fall? —
No.
Why not fly?

What if it goes wrong? —
No.
Why not let it go right?

What if they don't understand me?
—
No.
Why not be understood by myself
first?

I've spent too long in the world
of "what ifs",
tiptoeing around possibilities
like they were cracks in the
pavement.

But why not?

Why not leap before I'm ready?
Why not laugh so loud it echoes?
Why not be the only one who
believes,
if that's all it takes?

"What if" is a question.
"Why not" is a dare.
And I've decided —
I'm done asking.

Gema Garcia

I want to do it all —
every version of me that you see,
every version I dream of,
and most of all,
the version I was placed on this
earth to become.

I wasn't made by accident.
No heartbeat, no breath, no soul
is ever a mistake.
There is a reason I am here,
a purpose stitched into my being
like threads of gold running
through every vain.

I want to live up to all of it —
the wild hope, the quiet calling,
dreams too big to fit inside my
chest,

I want to chase it with both hands
open,
to be more than I was yesterday,
to be everything I was meant to be
tomorrow.

God doesn't craft creatures by
accident.
Every sunrise is intentional,
every tide moves with purpose.
And I —

I am no different.
So I will do it all.
Not perfectly.
Not without fear.
But with faith as my compass
and every potential inside me
waiting to be realized.

I can't wait to see who I become.

Gema Garcia

Stranger, though we've never met,

you've witnessed my innermost
thoughts,

my most vulnerable moments yet.

I hope you grasp the sincerity
behind these lines—

I'm cheering you on,

a silent ally in your life's
design.

When doubts creep in and fears
arise,

return to these pages,

and I hope my words can be a
guiding light.

From my perspective,

I assure you—

you possess the strength to
overcome,

to rise above,

to shine through.

Gema Garcia

ACKNOWLEDGMENTS

I've shared so much within these pages, so I'll keep this brief. If you think one of these poems is about you, you're probably right—thank you for the lessons taught.

To my family, I already expressed my gratitude at the start of this book, but now it's time to name-drop. Mom and Dad, thank you for shaping me into the resilient woman I am today. To my sisters—Shineah, Nashelie, and Genevieve—you hold my entire heart. Shelsie and Angelica, thank you for being the best built-in friends I could ever ask for. To my brother Morian, thank you for continuously restoring my faith in men and reminding me how I deserve to be treated.

Most importantly, to God: without Him, I wouldn't have survived the rebuilding of my heart. This book is an answer to my prayers. Thank you.

Gema Garcia

ABOUT THE AUTHOR

Gema is a 26-year-old author from Utah, celebrating the release of her debut book—a work that has been a long time in the making. By day, she works in a career outside the literary world. A traveler in heart, mind, and body, she draws inspiration from the richness of the world around her. Believing deeply that feelings deserve a place to be felt, this book is both a labor of love and an invitation for readers to embrace their own inner journeys.

Instagram: @_garcia.gema_

Gema Garcia